CW00499196

THE
POCKET

Irish
English

Published in 2024
by Gemini Adult Books Ltd
Part of Gemini Books Group

Based in Woodbridge and London
Marine House, Tide Mill Way
Woodbridge, Suffolk IP12 1AP
United Kingdom

www.geminibooks.com

Text and Design © 2024 Gemini Books Group
Part of the Gemini Pockets series

Cover image: szefei wong/Alamy Stock Photo

ISBN 978-1-91708-297-6

All rights reserved. No part of this publication may be reproduced in any
form or by any means – electronic, mechanical, photocopying, recording or
otherwise – or stored in any retrieval system of any nature without prior
written permission from the copyright holders.

A CIP catalogue record for this book is available from the British Library.

Disclaimer: The book is a guidebook purely for information and entertainment
purposes only. All trademarks, individual and company names, brand
names, registered names, quotations, celebrity names, logos, dialogues and
catchphrases used or cited in this book are the property of their respective
owners. The publisher does not assume and hereby disclaims any liability to
any party for any loss, damage or disruption caused by errors or omissions,
whether such errors or omissions result from negligence, accident or any other
cause. This book is an unofficial and unauthorized publication by Gemini Adult
Books Ltd and has not been licensed, approved, sponsored or endorsed by any
person or entity.

Printed in China

10 9 8 7 6 5 4 3 2 1

THE
POCKET

Irish
English

G:

Contents

Introduction

While it would be impossible to capture all the variety and richness of language of the country where just about everyone has the 'gift of the gab' and where that gift can be acquired or renewed simply by kissing the Blarney Stone, this charming book provides an excellent introduction, helping you to know your 'boreen' from your 'bodhrán', and your 'clochán' from your 'clock'. There are historical usages as well as many new entries which bring the book right up to date.

In Ireland, where nearly everyone is expert in the verbal arts, language is a very live, constantly changing phenomenon, more so than perhaps anywhere else. Not only is there the genius of individual invention to add variety, but also the legacy of the traditional occupations: the fishermen, shipbuilders, weavers, hill farmers and cattle rearers; the influence of the original language of the various settlers who have been transferred violently or peacefully to Ireland – the Scots, the West Country people, English Midlanders and returning Irish exiles from North America, Australia and elsewhere; and, of course, the Irish

language, Gaelic, itself. Each period of Irish history has also generated new words or new meanings for old words, and 'the Troubles' proved no exception.

Let's get started on learning to distinguish your 'banshees' from your 'bog sprites' and your 'boxty' from your 'champ'.

IRISH
–
ENGLISH

IRISH	ENGLISH
a (pron. *aah*)	letter 'a'
abroad	outside
acting the maggot	fooling around – 'Children, stop acting the maggot right now!'
ahint	behind
amadán	fool, idiot
annagh	marshy ground
annoy	upset
ard aighne (pron. *ordoyn*)	attorney general
ard fheis (pron. *orrd'esh*)	conference, general meeting (e.g., of a party)
arseways	the wrong way, also a bad result – 'the oul fella tried to make soda bread, but it went arseways.'
ath	ford
at oneself	all right

IRISH	ENGLISH
bad dose	a bad case of something – 'I got a pure bad dose of flu last year.'
bagsy	reserve – 'I bagsy the armchair for the game.'
baile	settlement or town
bake	face (Northern Ireland)

baloobas

drunk

The term baloobas, for being drunk, derives from the name of the Baluba people in what is now the Democratic Republic of the Congo. In 1960, in Niemba, Katanga Province, Irish troops serving with a United Nations peacekeeping mission were mistaken for mercenaries and ambushed by the Baluba. Nine Irish soldiers were killed.

Baile Átha Cliath

(pron. Balyehacloy)

Dublin

Meaning the 'town of the hurdled ford', this is the Irish name of the country's capital, Dublin. *Áth Cliath* is the name of a fording point on the River Liffey near Father Mathew Bridge. *Baile Átha Cliath* was an early Christian monastery, thought to be sited where Whitefriar Street Carmelite Church currently stands.

IRISH	ENGLISH
balla	wall
ballot	raffle
bally	town
bang on	good
banjaxed	not working, broken – 'The feckin' coffee machine is banjaxed again!'
banshee	lady of death, spirit appearing when a death is imminent
bap	bread roll, head
barn	fortified enclosure
barrer	wheelbarrow
beaker	mug

IRISH	ENGLISH
beamer	embarrassed – 'pulling a beamer' (Northern Ireland)
bean	woman
beour	girl or woman
big	close (of friends)
bleedin'	very, similar to 'bloody' in English – 'The weather's bleedin' freezing.'
bley	grey, ashen-looking
blow-in	someone who moves into a new area, whether from far away or not
boast	hollow
bodhrán (pron. *borán*)	hand drum, tambour
bogger	someone who lives in a remote part of Ireland. See also **culchie**

black stuff

Guinness (beer)

Guinness stout was first brewed in 1759 at
St James's Gate, Dublin. Today, it is brewed in
over forty countries and, in 2011, 850 million
litres (225 million US gallons) of Guinness were
sold worldwide. Although even current owner
Diageo refers to Guinness as the 'black stuff',
it is, in fact, a very deep ruby colour.

IRISH	ENGLISH
bogging	filthy
boke	vomit
bold	naughty
bollox, bollocks	literally testicles, but used to refer both to someone you dislike, but also a close friend – 'That fella's some bollox.'
Bord Fáilte (pron. *bord folchyeh*)	Tourist Board
boreen	lane, byroad
bothered	deaf
boxty	fried grated potatoes, flour and water
brave	good, of a crowd, game, etc.
brogue	accent
brutal	bad – 'I kissed another cailín – I feel brutal about it.'

IRISH	ENGLISH
buck eejit	a *very* stupid person
buckled	very drunk. See also **scuttered** and **locked**
bunse up	go equal shares on

broughan

porridge

Even prior to AD1500, oats and barley were staple foods in Ireland. Also called 'stirabout' in the past, porridge is an ancient Irish food.

IRISH	ENGLISH
cailín	girl
cailíní	girls
camogie	women's hurling
cant	auction
cat	unpleasant or difficult situation
catch oneself on	wise up, realise
cathedral	Catholic church
céad míle fáilte (pron. *kaydmeelyefoylcheh*)	welcome
céili(dh) (pron. *keylee*)	dance/informal evening of song and story
champ	mashed potatoes, scallions, butter, egg
chancer	a dishonest opportunist
chapel	Catholic church
chaps	mashed potato

IRISH	ENGLISH
cheeser	conker
chipper	fish-and-chip shop or other takeaway
chiseler	child
ciotóg	left-handed
clart	untidy person
class	good
clatter	pile, a lot – 'I've got a clatter of homework'
clem	steal
clochán	cairn; stone pavement (historical)
clock	beetle
clon	meadow
coddin' ya	kidding you – 'He's only coddin' ya' means 'He's only joking.'

IRISH	ENGLISH
cog (*v.*)	cheat, copy
collogue	collude in a whisper
come-all-ye	traditional musical get-together
cop on	understand, grow up
Córas lompair Éireann (CIE)	state transport organisation
cowp	overturn
cracking	brilliant
craic	fun. See also **minus craic**
crannóg	(ancient) lake dwelling
creamery can	milk churn
creel	basket, wicker barrier
creepie	low stool

Claddagh ring

friendship ring

A Claddagh ring, worn by both women and men, has two hands holding a crowned heart. The hands represent friendship, the heart, love, and the crown, loyalty. If worn on the left hand with the heart facing outwards, it shows that you are engaged. When the heart faces inwards on the same hand, it shows that you are married. If worn on the right hand with the heart facing outwards, you are still single, and looking for love; facing inwards on the right hand shows that you are in a committed relationship.

Croppy

*a nationalist rebel at the
end of eighteenth century*

The Croppies were Irish rebels who took part
in the Irish Rebellion of 1798, in sympathy with
the principles of the French Revolution. Their
name derived from their hair, which they wore
short in opposition to the powdered periwigs
worn by the Protestant Ascendancy. The rising
was defeated at the Battle of Vinegar Hill,
overlooking Enniscorthy in County Wexford,
on 21 June 1798, when 10,000 Crown troops
attacked and defeated the 20,000 rebels and
camp followers on the hill.

IRISH	ENGLISH
culchie	someone who lives in a remote part of Ireland. A Dubliner will think of any other Irish person as a culchie. See also **bogger**
Cumann Lúthchleas Gael	Gaelic Athletic Association
curach	coracle, canoe
cut	embarrassed, drunk
cute hoor	a crafty person – 'That fella's a cute hoor, always with a new cailín.'

IRISH	ENGLISH
Dáil (pron. *doyle*)	the lower house of the *Oireachtas*, the Irish parliament
dander	a walk, a stroll
deadly	Dublin slang for something good or great – 'We went out on the lash last night and the craic was deadly.'
deadly buzz	an exciting experience
dead on	great
deenee shee (*daoine sídh*)	good, fairy folk
delira and excira	an abbreviation of 'delighted and excited', an expression of happiness
dinneling	shiver, tremble
donagh	church
donkeys' years	a long time – 'I hadn't seen my old school friends in donkeys' years, not since I left Bandon in 2003.'

IRISH	ENGLISH
dope	a stupid person
doss	avoid work
dosser	a lazy person, someone avoiding work – 'Listen, you little dosser, get on with your work.'
dote	pet (*n.*), cute (of person)
down the country	in the countryside. **Boggers** and **culchies** live **down the country**.
drouthy	thirsty, parched
drouth (*n.*)	drinker
dryshite	someone who is boring or no fun
dulse	edible, reddish seaweed
duncher	flat cap

IRISH	ENGLISH
earwigging	listening in on someone else's conversation
eat the head off	scold in an aggressive manner
eejit	idiot (a mild insult) – 'feckin' eejit' makes for a more powerful insult. See also **spanner** and **tool**
effin' and blindin'	swearing – 'Me oul fella was effin' and blindin' when the car wouldn't start.'
ere yesterday	day before yesterday
evening	afternoon
failing	losing weight, in poor health
fair play	'well done', said in response to the slightest achievement or something done well – 'Fair play to you!'
farl (soda, wheaten, etc.)	type of griddle bread
fear	man

Éire

(pron. *aira*)

Ireland

Éire is how Ireland is named in Irish Gaelic.
Between 1937 and 1949 it was the official
name of the Republic of Ireland.

fear dearg (far darrig)

hobgoblin, mischievous prankster

Fear dearg means 'red man' as the hobgoblin is supposed to wear a red coat and cap. They are also known as 'rat boys', described as being fat, having dark, hairy skin, pronounced snouts and thin tails. A far darrig is solitary, like a leprechaun, and likes to play practical jokes, sometimes gruesome ones, sometimes substituting changelings for babies. They are thought by some to be linked to nightmares.

IRISH	ENGLISH
feck	a coy version of fuck
fecker	a term of abuse for someone
feek	a term of endearment for an attractive person
feis (pron. fesh)	dancing or music competition
fella	a male – 'The fellas went out on the lash last night.'
fernenst	opposite
fierce	very, extremely – 'It's fierce busy in town.'
fine	sometimes an expression, like **grand**, to deter further discussion, but can also be used to describe someone attractive – 'She's a fine thing.'
fornint	in front of
fir	men (as seen on toilet doors)

IRISH	ENGLISH
flah	boast, show off
Fleadh Cheoil (pron. *flahkyol*)	an annual arts festival and competition run by Comhaltas Ceoltóirí Éireann
flute	mild curse, equivalent to 'flip' in English
fluthered	drunk
foostering	fussing without accomplishing much – 'There was a lot of foostering about, but nothing really achieved.'
football	Gaelic football or rugby union
form	mood, spirits
foundered	freezing (of persons and animals)
Free State	term sometimes used to denote the Republic of Ireland

IRISH	ENGLISH
fussed	be bothered, to care
futter	fidget
futtery	fidgety

fry
traditional Irish breakfast

Called an 'Ulster fry' in Northern Ireland, an Irish 'fry' differs from 'a full English' by including black or white pudding and soda bread, farls or boxty.

IRISH	ENGLISH
Gaelic	Irish language
Gaelic Athletic Association (GAA)	*Cumann Lúthchleas Gael*, the umbrella organisation for Irish sports
Gaeltacht	Gaelic-speaking areas
gaff	home
gag	laugh, funny person
gammy	injured, sore
Garda	police officer
Garda Síochána	national police and security service of Ireland
Gardaí	'the Guards', the police
gas	funny (of a person or situation), also used to express shock or disbelief
gauger	excise man
gawk	stare

IRISH	ENGLISH
geebag	a term of abuse for a woman – 'That Mrs O'Reilly's a pure geebag.'
get on me, you, him, etc.	get dressed
get off me, you, him, etc.	get undressed
giddy	giggly, light-hearted
gimme a shot	let me use – 'Gimme a shot of your surfboard.'
give it a lash	give something a go – 'I've never made soda bread before. I thought I'd give it a lash.'
giving out	complaining, ranting – 'Me wife was giving out to me for getting scuttered.'
gobdaw	a foolish or stupid person
gobshite	a foolish person

IRISH	ENGLISH
gombeen, gombeen man (*gaimbín*)	shady, small time wheeler-dealer, in business or politics, also an idiot
gorb	person who eats a lot
gowl	a person you dislike
grá	love, also passion or desire – 'She has a grá for camogie.'
grand	okay, fine, adequate, but could also mean 'absolutely dreadful'
gravy ring	ring doughnut
great	close (of friends)
guff	excuses, disrespect
gunk	disappointment, surprise
g'wan	'go on', an expression of enthusiasm or encouragement

gutties

trainers, plimsolls

In Northern Ireland, also Scotland, gym shoes, plimsolls or trainers were called gutties, from gutta-percha, the plastic substance derived from the tree of the same name. In Malay, *getah* translates as 'latex' and *perca* means 'scrap' or 'rag'. In Limerick, trainers are sometimes called 'tackies' a word brought back from South Africa by a returning priest.

IRISH	ENGLISH
half'un	short (spirit measure)
hallion	a useless person, a rogue – 'Yer man is a fierce hallion.'
hames	mess, something done in clumsy way – 'He made a real hames of that kick.'
hammered	drunk
heel	crust of a piece of bread, end of a piece of cheese, etc.
herself, himself	he, she
hinch	thigh
hoke	rummage
holy show	mess, disaster
hot press	airing cupboard
hurley, hurling stick	stick used in hurling
hurling	A Gaelic sport played with sticks (hurleys), a sliotar (hurling ball) and goals

hooley

raucous party

Commonly used in Ireland, hooley (or hoolie) for a raucous party is said to be derived from Orkney Scots, where the same word means a strong wind or gale.

IRISH	ENGLISH
ignorant	rude
in a heap	hungover
in a hoop	hungover
in bits	in a bad way – 'My head was in bits this morning after I got scuttered last night.'
in ribbons	in a bad way – 'He's in a heap, his head's in ribbons.'
Irish	Irish whiskey, as in 'a drink of Irish'
jackeen	Dubliner – 'Ignore him, he's just a jackeen who thinks we're all boggers.'
jacks, the	the toilet
jag	injection, to prick

Janey Mack

euphemism for 'Jesus Christ'

Janey Mack appears as an expression
in James Joyce's *Ulysses*, published in 1922,
but is thought to have been first used in 1914,
in the *Catholic Bulletin* – '"Oh, Janey Mack,
she's mad," said Custhard-Puss.'

Jesus, Mary and Joseph

an expression of frustration or irritation

Jesus, Mary and Joseph was famously
embellished as 'Jesus, Mary and Joseph
and the wee donkey!' by fictional character
Superintendent Ted Hastings, played by Adrian
Dunbar, in TV police drama *Line of Duty*.

IRISH	ENGLISH
jagger	nip, twinge, prickle
jammers	very crowded, full
jammy	lucky
japped	splashed (with mud, etc.)
Jaysus!	Jesus! exclamation of shock or surprise
jo maxi	taxi
juke	look furtively at, get out of, avoid
jumper	sweater

IRISH	ENGLISH
keen	eager, enthusiastic
keen (*caoine*)	lamentation, to lament loudly
keener	professional lamenter
keep someone going	have someone on
kip	a messy or dirty place – 'That oul fella's house is a complete kip.'
kitchen	relish (*n.*), use sparingly
knackered	exhausted
langer	a stupid person (Cork slang)
langers	drunk – 'He was completely langers last Friday', also 'langered'
lash	quick movement – 'We're late for school, give yourself a lash' – also, an attractive person – 'That cailín is a lash.'
leaping	stinking, filthy

IRISH	ENGLISH
leg it	run away – 'Quick! The Gardaí are coming. Leg it!'
length	as far as – as in 'the length of'
lepping	throbbing
leprechaun	small, mischievous supernatural being, usually depicted as a little bearded man, wearing a coat and hat
liúdramán	wastrel, lout
lift	take away, arrest
lig	foolish person
line	date – 'to do a line with someone'
lob the gob	kiss
locked	very drunk. See also **buckled** and **scuttered**
look	want
lough	lake

IRISH	ENGLISH
manky	disgusting, dirty, rotten – 'The weather has been manky all week.'
meeting	kissing – 'Will you meet him tonight?' See also **shifting**
melter	an annoying person – 'That fella I used to go out with is a fierce melter.'
merrow	mermaid
middle shed	centre parting
minch	trespass
minerals	soft drinks – Irish grandparents like to offer a mineral, usually 7 Up, and they don't like to be refused
minus craic	the opposite of **craic** (fun)
mitch	truant

messages, the

groceries

The messages, for 'groceries', derives from
when people would get their telegrams
and letters from the post office, where they
also bought their groceries.

mummer

person in disguise

While a mummer can mean simply a person
in disguise, mumming is a masking or
masquerade tradition which still exists in
many parts of Ireland. As well as masquerade,
a traditional play with stock characters –
many of them derived from the European
carnival tradition – is performed.

IRISH	ENGLISH
mná	women (as seen on toilet doors)
moran	fool
mot	girlfriend
mouldy	drunk
muck	pig
mullered	drunk
muppet	foolish person
mustard	lively, into everything

IRISH	ENGLISH
naggin	a small bottle of spirits, typically vodka
nixer	casual job
noggin	wooden mug, drink measure
notion, to take a notion on	fancy (*n.* and *v.*)
nuacht (pron. *newoght*)	news (on radio, TV, etc.)
off your head	drunk
ogeous handling	tricky situation
Oireachtas	Irish parliament
old (pron. *ole*)	general terms denoting despisal or endearment
old year's night	new year's eve
on the lash	drinking – 'They were out on the lash every night last week.'
ossified	drunk
oul dear	mother
oul fella	father, or any older man

notions

delusions of grandeur

Notions translates loosely as having delusions of grandeur or, perhaps more accurately, simply aspiring to be middle class. Examples of 'notions' might include: paying €100 for a haircut; employing a cleaner; doing Pilates or yoga; drinking any tea other than Barry's, or drinking Barry's black; or having an English-sounding surname.

IRISH	ENGLISH
oul wan	mother
out of your tree	drunk
own	family, as in 'one's own'
oxter	armpit
oxtercog	carry someone by supporting them under the arms

IRISH	ENGLISH
pan	soft white loaf. See **sliced pan**
pass oneself	behave reasonably, not make a fool of oneself
pastie	deep-fried minced meat and potatoes
peeler	police officer, copper
picky	finicky
pictures	film, movie
piece	packed lunch
planxty	slow jig
plugher	cough
poke	cone, ice cream cornet
powerful	extremely (a superlative)
poxy	not great, not working, also a swearword – 'I couldn't get the poxy car to start.'
press	cupboard

poteen (poitín)

(pron. *pacheen*)

illicitly distilled spirits

Poitín derives its name from its literal meaning, a 'small pot', in which *poitín* was traditionally made, usually in remote rural areas to evade the police. Also known as 'Irish moonshine' and 'mountain dew', *poitín* was produced in New York's Irishtown by the growing Irish diaspora.

IRISH	ENGLISH
prog	provisions (food), to steal
puck	punch
punt	Irish pound (old currency)
pure	similar to **fierce**, but more extreme – 'It's been pure wet all week.'
puss	sulky face
put on me, you, him, etc.	get dressed
put over	put by, save
quality	very good
quare	very, unusually
quilt	objectionable person
rag order	a very bad condition – 'The house was in rag order after that party.'
rapid	Dublin slang for something **deadly**

IRISH	ENGLISH
Raidió Teilifís Éireann (RTE)	Irish public-service broadcaster
rath	hill fort
read intil oneself	read silently, to oneself
red up	tidy up, put in order
remark	notice
rightly	well, drunk

Púcaí (púca, puck)

goblin, animal spirit

Púcaí are creatures of Celtic, English and Channel Islands folklore. They were thought to bring both good luck and misfortune. *Púcaí* are believed to have dark or white fur and to be able to take on the appearance of animals such as horses, goats, cats, dogs, hares or even human form, though with animal ears or a tail.

IRISH	ENGLISH
sally	willow
sap	a fool
sauncy	lively, jolly (girl)
savage	good
scalded (heartscalded)	distressed, upset
scallion	spring onion
scarlet	embarrassed
scoop	a pint or other alcoholic drink – 'Your man went out for a few scoops last nigh.'
scrab	scratch
scran	bad luck – 'Bad scran to you.'
scratcher	bed
scundered	embarrassed or uncomfortable
scuttered	very drunk. See also **buckled** and **locked**

IRISH	ENGLISH
Seanad (pron. *shonad*)	Senate, the upper house of the *Oireachtas*, the Irish parliament
seisiún	session (of music or dance)
shaper	someone walking with a pronounced strut
shaping	walking in a cocky way, like a **shaper**
shaugh	ditch
shebeen (*síbín*)	unlicensed drinking venue
shed	parting (in the hair)

Scut

a waster, also a stupid person

Scut is said to be derived from 'scut work',
an old-fashioned term for manual labour.

IRISH	ENGLISH
shifting	kissing – 'Will you shift her tonight?' See also **meeting**
shillelagh	blackthorn cudgel
shired	take a break, as in 'get one's head shired'
shitehawk	contemptible person
shook	hungover – 'He's as shook as a hand at mass.'
shoulder	a large bottle of spirits, typically vodka
siamsa (pron. *shomsa*)	amusement, entertainment
simmit	undervest
skitter	frivolous, contemptible person
skyte	to strike with a sharp or glancing blow
slag	insult someone, but in a way which isn't usually intended to hurt their feelings

IRISH	ENGLISH
sláinte (pron. *slancher*)	cheers, to your good health
slap	gap, in hedge, etc.
sleeveen	sly, calculating person
slieve	mountain
sleutery	limp, lame
sliced pan	sliced white bread, an Irish staple
slip	young, or slim, girl
slope	saunter, ramble
soft weather	mild weather
sorry?	a response to a question which has made you angry
sound	thank you – 'Sound for giving me a lift home.'
spanner	idiot. See also **tool** and **eejit**

spailpín

lad, migratory labourer

A *spailpín* was an itinerant or seasonal farmworker from the seventeenth to the early twentieth century. The Irish word *spailp* means 'turn', 'spell' or 'bout'.

IRISH	ENGLISH
speel	clamber, climb
spitting	light rain – 'It's only spitting.'
spud	potato
stall the ball	hang on, wait – 'Stall the ball, I'll be ready in five minutes.'
stocious	very drunk
stooked	very tired, exhausted
stop the lights!	I don't believe you!
streel	trail, untidy mess
suckin' diesel	making progress – 'This was going nowhere yesterday, but now we're suckin' diesel.'
suit	it suits one – 'to suit it'
sure look	a filler expression, a suggestion of things being beyond one's control – 'Sure look, I know things aren't grand.'

IRISH	ENGLISH
tae	tea, as in *cupán tae*
taig	a Catholic (derogatory), an English form of the Irish male name Tadhg, used in Northern Ireland by loyalists as a derogatory term for Catholics.
Taoiseach (pron. *teeshogh*)	the prime minister of Ireland
teach ceoil (pron. *chogh kyole*)	village music hall
Teachta Dála (TD) (pron. *choghtadola*)	member of the Irish parliament, the Dáil Éireann, the lower house of the *Oireachtas* (an MP)
thaveless	incompetent
thick	close (of friends), also 'stupid'
throughother	disorganised
tint	small quantity of

Tír na nÓg

(pron. *cheeman oog*)

mystical land of youth

Tír na nÓg, which means 'land of the young', is a name in Irish mythology for the Celtic otherworld, a realm where the gods, other supernatural beings and the dead exist.

tosspot

a term of abuse

Borrowed from England, tosspot is a
term for someone one dislikes. Originally,
the word described a heavy drinker in days
when beer was served in clay pots, which
the drinker would toss back.

IRISH	ENGLISH
tool	idiot, as in a blunt object. See also **spanner** and **eejit**
topper	great lad or girl
torture	tease, annoy
tovy	boastful
townland	district

tricolour, the

the Irish national flag

During the nineteenth century, various
flags came to symbolise Irish nationalism,
including a gold harp on a green background.
Many of them included green (for Roman
Catholics), orange for Protestants (supporters
of William of Orange) and white for hoped-for
peace between them. The modern tricolour
was constitutionally recognised on
29 December 1937.

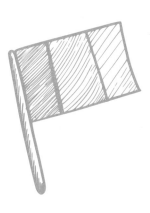

U W Y

IRISH	ENGLISH
uilleann pipes	Irish bagpipes
unbeknownst	unknown to, without knowing
unreal	good
up to 90	extremely busy – 'Liam, could you get the door, please? I'm up to 90 here.'
up to high doh	excited
wagon	a girl or woman acting in a particular way – 'She was behaving like a right wagon when she got locked last night.'
wains	small children
weather	these days, nowadays, as in 'this weather'
wheeker	really good
whenever	when
whiskey	Irish whiskey

water sheerie

will o' the wisp

Also known as 'bog sprites', water sheeries appear as lights which hover over a bog and can look like a far-off candle, sometimes luring an unwary traveller to a house which doesn't exist and a watery grave, for which reason they are also known as 'corpse candles'. Anaerobic bacteria digest organic material to produce a gas called phosphine, which is able to spontaneously combust. Will o' the wisp or *Ignis fatuus* – despite its other name, 'foolish fire' – is a real phenomenon: a ball of flame that hovers above a bog's dark, still water for a few minutes before disappearing.

Yellaman

a type of sweet

Yellaman, or yellowman, is a bright
yellow, chewy, toffee-like honeycomb made
in Northern Ireland. The sweet is particularly
associated with the Ould Lammas Fair
in Ballycastle, County Antrim.

IRISH	ENGLISH
whopper	amazing, great, incredible
wick	useless, rotten
wired up	crazy
yer man	a man you don't know, or you don't much like
yer one	a reference to someone one doesn't know – 'Who is yer one standing in the corner?'
yer wan	a woman you don't know, or don't much like
yet	still
yoke	thing, 'thingamajig', 'doodah' – 'I can't find that poxy yoke for the dishwasher.'
yonks	a very long time – 'Jesus, Mary, Joseph and the wee donkey! We haven't got scuttered together for yonks!'

ENGLISH
–
IRISH

ENGLISH	IRISH
absolutely dreadful	grand
accent	brogue
adequate	grand
afternoon	evening
airing cupboard	hot press
all right	at oneself
amazing	whopper
amusement	siamsa
angry response	sorry?
annoying person	mutter
armpit	oxter
arrest	take away
as far as	length
ashen-looking	bley
attorney general	*ard aighne*
attractive person	lash
auction	cant
avoid	juke
avoid work	doss

ENGLISH	IRISH
bad	brutal
bad case	bad dose
bad luck	scran
bad result	arseways
basket	creel
be bothered	fussed
bed	scratcher
beetle	clock
behave reasonably	pass oneself
behind	ahint
blackthorn cudgel	shillelagh
bloody	bleedin'
boast	flah
boastful	tovy
boring person	dryshite
bread roll	bap
brilliant	cracking
broken	banjaxed
byroad	boreen

ENGLISH	IRISH
cairn	*clochán*
canoe	curach
carry someone under the arms	oxtercog
casual job	nixer
Catholic (derogatory)	taig
Catholic church	cathedral chapel
centre parting	middle shed
cheat	cog
cheers	*sláinte*
child	chiseler
church	donagh
clamber	speel
close (of friends)	big thick
close friend	bollocks bollox
collude in a whisper	collogue
complaining	giving out
conference	*ard fheis*

conker	cheeser
contemptible person	shitehawk
copy	cog
coracle	curach
cough	plugher
crafty person	cute hoor
crazy	wired up
crust of bread	heel
cupboard	press

ENGLISH	IRISH
dance	*céili(dh)*
dancing or music competition	*feis*
date (*v.*)	line
day before yesterday	ere yesterday
deaf	bothered
delighted and excited	delira and excira
delusions of grandeur	notions
desire	*grá*
difficult situation	cat

dirty	manky
disappointment	gunk
disaster	holy show
disgusting	manky
dishonest opportunist	chancer
district	townland
ditch	shaugh
drink measure	noggin
drinker	drouth
drinking	on the lash
drunk	baloobas
	cut
	fluthered
	hammered
	langered
	langers
	mouldy
	mullered
	off your head
	ossified
	out of your tree
	rightly
drunk, very	locked
	scuttered
	stocious
	buckled
Dublin	*Baile Átha Cliath*
Dubliner	jackeen

ENGLISH	IRISH
eager	keen
edible, reddish seaweed	dulse
embarrassed	beamer
	cut
	scarlet
	scundered
entertainment	siamsa
excise man	gauger
excited	up to high doh
exciting experience	deadly buzz
excuses	guff
exhausted	knackered
	stooked
expression of frustration, irritation	Jesus, Mary and Joseph
extremely	fierce
	powerful
	pure
extremely busy	up to 90

ENGLISH	IRISH
face	bake
family	own
father	oul fella
fidget	futter
fidgety	futtery
film	pictures
filthy	bogging
	leaping
fine	grand
finicky	picky
fish-and-chip shop	chipper
flat cap	duncher
folk festival	*Fleadh Cheoil*
fool	*amadán*
	moran
	sap
fooling around	acting the maggot
foolish person	gobshite
	lig
	muppet
ford	ath

fortified enclosure	barn
freezing	foundered
fried grated potatoes, flour and water	boxty
friendship ring	Claddagh ring
frivolous, contemptible person	skitter
fuck	feck
full	jammers
fun	craic
funny	gas
funny person	gag
fussing without accomplishing much	foostering

ENGLISH	IRISH
Gaelic Athletic Association (GAA)	*Cumann Lúthchleas Gael*
Gaelic football	football
Gaelic-speaking areas	*Gaeltacht*
gap, in hedge, etc.	slap

general meeting	*ard fheis*
get dressed	get on me, you, him, etc.
	put on me, you, him, etc.
get out of	juke
get undressed	get off me, you, him, etc.
giggly	giddy
girl	beour
	cailín
girl or woman behaving badly	wagon
girlfriend	mot
girls	*cailíní*
give something a go	give it a lash
go equal shares on	bunse up
good	bang on
	brave
	class
	deadly
	savage
good, fairy folk	deenee shee
great	dead on
	whopper
great girl, lad	topper
grey	bley
griddle bread	farl
groceries	the messages
grow up	cop on
Guinness	black stuff

ENGLISH	IRISH
hair parting	shed
hand drum	*bodhrán*
hang on	stall the ball
have someone on	keep someone going
he	himself
head	bap
hill fort	rath
hobgoblin	far darrig
hollow	boast
home	gaff
hungover	in a heap
	in a hoop
	shook

ENGLISH	IRISH
ice cream cone, cornet	poke
idiot	*amadán*
	eejit
	gombeen
	spanner
	tool
in a bad way	in bits
	in ribbons
in front of	fornint
in poor health	failing
in the countryside	down the country
incompetent	thaveless
incredible	whopper
informal evening of song and story	*céili(dh)*
injection	jag
injured	gammy
insult someone, kindly	slag
into everything	mustard
Ireland	*Éire*
Irish bagpipes	uilleann pipes
Irish language	Gaelic

Irish national flag	tricolour
Irish national police service	*Garda Síochána*
Irish parliament	*Oireachtas*
Irish parliament (the lower house)	*Dáil*
Irish pound (old currency)	punt
Irish sports organisation	Gaelic Athletic Association (GAA)
Irish state broadcaster	*Raidió Teilifís Éireann* (RTE)
Irish whiskey	Irish

ENGLISH	IRISH
Jesus!	Jaysus!
Jesus Christ!	Janey Mack!
jolly (of a girl)	sauncy

ENGLISH	IRISH
kidding you	coddin' ya
kiss	lob the gob
kissing	shifting

ENGLISH	IRISH
lad	spalpeen
lady of death	banshee
lake	lough
lake dwelling	*crannóg*
lame	sleutery
lamentation	keen
lane	boreen
large bottle of spirits	shoulder
laugh	gag

lazy person	dosser
left-handed	*ciotóg*
let me use	gimme a shot
light rain	spitting
limp	sleutery
listening in on someone	earwigging
lively	mustard
lively (of a girl)	saucy
long time	donkeys' years
look furtively at	juke
losing weight	failing
lot	clatter
lout	*liúdramán*
love	*grá*
low stool	creepie
lucky	jammy

ENGLISH	IRISH
male	fella
man	fear

man you don't know/ don't much like	yer man
marshy ground	annagh
mashed potato, scallion, butter, egg	chaps
mashed potatoes	champ
meadow	clon
member of the Irish parliament	*Teachta Dála* (TD)
men	*fir*
mermaid	merrow
mess	holy show
messy place	kip
migratory labourer	spalpeen
mild curse	flute
milk churn	creamery can
mood	form
mother	oul dear
	oul wan
mountain	slieve
movie	pictures
mug	beaker
mystical land of youth	*Tír na nÓg*

ENGLISH	IRISH
nationalist rebel	Croppy
naughty	bold
new year's eve	old year's night
news (on radio, TV, etc.)	nuacht
not fun	minus craic
not great	poxy
not make a fool of oneself	pass oneself
notice	remark
objectionable person	quilt
okay	grand
older man	oul fella
opposite	fernenst
outside	abroad
overturn	cowp

ENGLISH	IRISH
parched	drouthy
passion	*grá*
person in disguise	mummer
person you dislike	gowl
person who eats a lot	gorb
pet	dote
pig	muck
pint of beer (or other alcoholic drink)	scoop
plimsolls	gutties
police	*Gardaí*
police officer	*Garda*
	peeler
porridge	broughan
potato	spud
	cupboard
prime minister of Ireland	*Taoiseach*
provisions (food)	prog
punch	puck
put in order	red up

ENGLISH	IRISH
quick movement	lash

ENGLISH	IRISH
raffle	ballot
ramble	slope
ranting	giving out
read silently	read intil oneself
realise	catch oneself on
really good	wheeker
relish (*n.*)	kitchen
Republic of Ireland	Free State
reserve	bagsy
rind of cheese	heel
ring doughnut	gravy ring
rogue	hallion

rotten	manky
rude	ignorant
rugby union	football
rummage	hoke
run away	leg it

ENGLISH	IRISH
saunter	slope
save	put over
scold in an aggressive manner	eat the head off
scratch	scrab
Senate	*Seanad*
session	*seisiún*
settlement	*baile*
shady, small time wheeler-dealer	gombeen (man)
she	herself
shiver	dinneling
short (spirit measure)	half'un
show off	flah

slow jig	planxty
sly, calculating person	sleeveen
small children	wains
small quantity of	tint
small, mischievous supernatural being	leprechaun
soft drinks	minerals
soft white loaf	pan
someone from a remote part of Ireland	bogger culchie
someone from elsewhere	blow-in
someone one doesn't know	yer one
someone who struts	shaper
someone you dislike	bollocks, bollox
sore	gammy
spirit when a death is imminent	banshee
spirits	form
splashed	japped
spring onion	scallion
stare	gawk
state transport organisation	*Córas Iompair Éireann* (CIE)
steal	clem
stick used in hurling	hurley, hurling stick
still	yet
stone pavement	*clochán*

stroll	dander
stupid	thick
stupid person	dope
	eejit
	gobdaw
	langer
	puss
stupid person, very	buck eejit
surprise	gunk
swearing	effin' and blindin'

ENGLISH	IRISH
take a break	shired
takeaway	chipper
taxi	jo maxi
tea	*tae*
tease	torture
term of abuse	fecker
	tosspot
term of abuse for a woman	geebag
term of endearment	feek
thank you	sound

the wrong way	arseways
these days	weather
thigh	hinch
thing	yoke
thirsty	drouthy
throbbing	lepping
tidy up	red up
to care	fussed
to lament loudly	keen
to prick	jag
to steal	prog
to strike with a sharp or glancing blow	skyte
toilet	the jacks
Tourist Board	*Bord Fáilte*
town	*baile*
	bally
traditional Irish breakfast	fry
traditional musical get-together	come-all-ye
trail	streel
trainers	gutties
tremble	dinneling
trespass	minch
tricky situation	ogeous handling
truant	mitch
twinge	jagger

ENGLISH	IRISH
uncomfortable	scundered
understand	cop on
unknown to	unbeknownst
unlicensed drinking venue	shebeen
unpleasant situation	cat
untidy mess	streel
untidy person	clart
unusually	quare
upset	annoy
use sparingly	kitchen
useless person	hallion

ENGLISH	IRISH
very	fierce
very bad condition	rag order

very crowded	jammers
very good	rapid
	quality
very long time	yonks
very tired	stooked
village music hall	*teach ceoil*
vomit	boke

ENGLISH	IRISH
wait	stall the ball
walk	dander
walking in a cocky way	shaping
wall	balla
want	look
wastrel	*liúdramán*
welcome	*céad míle fáilte*
well	rightly
well done	fair play
wheelbarrow	barrer
when	whenever
wicker barrier	creel

will o' the wisp	water sheerie
willow	sally
wise up	catch oneself on
without knowing	unbeknownst
woman	bean
	beour
women	*mná*
woman you don't know or much like	yer wan
women's hurling	camogie
wooden mug	noggin

ENGLISH   **IRISH**

yellowman (a type of sweet)	yellaman
young, or slim, girl	slip

IRISH
IDIOMS

IRISH	ENGLISH
Ah, here!	an expression of outrage – 'Ah, here! I'm sick of this manky weather!'
Bout ye?	Northern Irish slang for 'How are you?'
C'mere to me	'Come here to me', meaning 'Listen to me' or 'I've got something to tell you.'
Don't bother your barney about it	Don't bother/mind about it
Fair play to you!	Well done!
fierce mild	'It's a fierce mild day. I'm down to my T-shirt.'
Get outta that garden	Stop it, I don't believe you
Get up outta that	I don't believe you
give someone the nyrps	depress someone
good day for drying	a nice dry day with a bit of a breeze, good for hanging the clothes on the line

IRISH	ENGLISH
G'way outta that	expresses disbelief (in response to a compliment, for example), similar to 'don't be silly' or 'it's no trouble'
Houl yer whisht	Be quiet
How's-a-going?	How is it going?
How's she cuttin'?	a greeting, similar to 'How's it going?' or 'How are you?'
How's the form?	How are you getting on?
It's a day for the fire	a cold day
It's wetter than Michael Phelps's pocket	a very wet day
I will, yeah	I certainly won't
not the full shilling	not fully sane
on the tear	out drinking
put something on the long finger	put something off
put the arm/hand in	fleece someone

IRISH	ENGLISH
soft day	misty with light rain
Story horse?	Dublin slang for 'How's it going?
take the headstaggers	go crazy
the craic was 90	it was great fun – 'After Cork won the hurling, the craic was 90.'
the sun is splitting the stones	it's a sunny day
to be at oneself	to be feeling okay
to be only after doing something	to have just done something
to have come down in the last shower	to be naive
Will I, yeah? or I will, yeah?	a response to an instruction one intends to ignore – 'Clean the house? I will, yeah?!'

IRISH	ENGLISH
your only man/woman	the right person for the job – 'You need your roof fixing? Seamus is your only man!'
You suit your hair long	Long hair suits you

PICTURE CREDITS

Alamy Stock Photo: szefei wong, 3. **Freepik.com:** 4, 5, 7, 9, 14, 17, 26, 36, 45, 49, 53, 64, 82, 89, 124. **Shutterstock:** OlgaChernyak, 19; WebbiMemo, 35; darko m, 39; Elen Kloss, 54; Kate Macate, 63; Yevheniia Lytvynovych, 73; yovannah, 87; Qualit Design, 94.